This journal belongs to:

_____

"If there ever comes a day when we can't be together, keep me in your heart. I'll stay there forever."
— A.A. Milne

Things to Remember Before I Forget

My Plan for My Care

Niki Tucker *and* Jenna Tucker Landry
FOREWORD BY TEEPA SNOW

WITH ILLUSTRATIONS BY EAMON MORRIS

LUMINARE PRESS
WWW.LUMINAREPRESS.COM

Things To Remember Before I Forget: My Plan for My Care
Copyright © 2022 by Niki Tucker and Jenna Tucker Landry

All rights reserved. This book or any portion thereof may not be reproduced or used in any manner whatsoever without the express written permission of the publisher, except for the use of brief quotations in a book review.

Printed in the United States of America

Luminare Press
442 Charnelton St.
Eugene, OR 97401
www.luminarepress.com

LCCN: 2022901334
ISBN: 978-1-64388-937-5

For Beverly Rowles, mother and grandmother, who supported, inspired, encouraged, and loved her family. You are greatly missed.

Contents

Foreword 1
Introduction 3
About Me 7
My Preferences 19
Daily Routine 29
Health and Wellness 35
My Life 45
Memory Loss 51
When I Need Care 59
Final Days 67
After I'm Gone 71
Last Words 77

Addendums

Technology 87
Doctors' Visits 93
Medication List 105
Diary 115
Acknowledgements by Niki 131
Acknowledgements by Jenna 132

Foreword

As an occupational therapist and dementia care educator with over forty years of experience working with those living with brain change, I have seen firsthand that many lifelong personality traits and preferences remain the same even after someone is diagnosed with dementia. Although some preferences may indeed shift or alter, far more remain consistent. Favorite foods, beverages, songs, and leisure activities, for example, often remain consistent throughout the various states of brain change, and serve as valuable ways for care partners to provide measures of comfort or moments of joy. Conversely, dislikes or intolerances may trigger distress, so knowledge of these is essential.

Things to Remember Before I Forget: My Plan for My Care provides an extremely valuable approach to documenting these personal preferences. The journaling style, with interspersed narratives, is an engaging format for capturing these details. The documented information about the individual will be a beneficial tool for care partners to use throughout the journey of dementia, and can serve as a living document to be adjusted and modified as needed. And, when the journey has ended, the book will provide a poignant legacy of the individual that may be cherished.

Teepa Snow, MS, OTR/L, FAOTA
Founder, Positive Approach to Care®

Introduction

Niki's thoughts:

My daughter Jenna and I went to a bookstore recently and purchased a guided journal meant for mothers and daughters to share. We have always had a close relationship and we thought this would be something fun to do together.

One night I was reading what she had written in her section. I smiled at some of her entries. Even at twenty-four years old, she could still surprise me with an unexpected comment. As I got ready for bed, I pondered the journal and what I was going to add next.

I pulled on my pajama top—never the pajama pants—and climbed into bed. As I did, I thought to myself, *I hate the feeling when my pajamas twist around my legs or get caught in the sheets. I should let Jenna know, just in case she ever has to get me ready for bed.*

At nearly 60, I knew there could come a day when that would be the case. Then my rational brain took over and I laughed. How likely was she to remember my pajama preference in twenty years? Maybe I should write it down for her.

And then the light bulb went on, sparking the idea for this journal. I immediately hopped out of bed, pulled on the pajama pants, and raced into her room.

"Jenna," I said, "we have to write a book!"

Jenna's thoughts:

Since my preteen years, I had wanted to be a writer. I spent hours with my notebooks and pencils, dreaming of characters in imaginary lands and wondering how I would bring them to life. It had never occurred to me to write a journal until my mom came into my room, bursting with excitement about her idea for writing a journal for those with memory loss. Her excitement was contagious and immediately I knew this was a great idea.

I had spent five years at a retirement community working with senior citizens at various stages of dementia. The facility provided care plans that only covered basic details and sometimes what the resident would have wanted might have been different than what the management and family said. A journal like the one my mother envisioned would have taken the mystery out of providing desired care, especially for care partners working with residents who had lost the ability to communicate or properly describe their needs.

My hope for the writers using this journal is that it will provide some peace. Those who are going through the difficult process of losing their memory might feel better, knowing that they have left details for their loved ones and caregivers to follow. For the families and caregivers who use this book, I hope the information provided will give you better understanding and appreciation for the one who needs care.

WHEN THE IDEA FOR THIS JOURNAL FIRST CAME TO NIKI, THE thought was to benefit those who had been recently diagnosed with dementia so they could make a plan for their care. But after spending several months adding, changing, and editing, Niki realized this isn't just a journal for those in the early stages of dementia, but for everyone who is aging and wants to plan ahead.

Be aware that there is no correct way to complete this journal. In fact, it may seem rather overwhelming with all the questions. Do not think you must answer everything but instead focus on the areas that are important to you.

You may also want to do some easy parts first—likes and dislikes are generally things you know well and can easily answer. Preferences for care may take a bit more thought and you may come back to it at a later time.

At the end of each chapter is a "check in" section. This is a place to write your thoughts and feelings on the day you completed that part of the journal. Use this to share with your family what you were thinking or feeling as you worked through this journal.

There are four general sections at the back of the book. One is a place to keep track of doctor appointments—when you went, who you saw, and what was covered at the appointment. The third section is for your medication list. Keep it current, note what is working for you and what you've tried that did not work. The fourth section is filled with blank pages for traditional journaling where you may share whatever comes to mind. You can do this daily, monthly, or whenever the mood strikes.

In reading this journal, you may note that instead of the term "caregiver", the words "care partner" are used. This terminology is recommended by Teepa Snow's Positive Approach to Care, and indicates that the relationship of caregiver and care receiver is not one-sided, but rather a partnership, working together to preserve quality of life, health, and dignity.

THIS JOURNAL IS NOT INTENDED TO TAKE THE PLACE OF legal documents. Please consult an attorney for any advance directives necessary.

~~This chapter is a place where you can record important~~ aspects of your personality, preferences, habits, likes, and dislikes. Reflecting on past events may help to answer some of these questions.

For example, when Jenna and Niki went to the bookstore, Niki was browsing the books on aging and when she looked up, she realized Jenna was gone. She felt a moment of panic. The tall bookcases blocked her view, people were coming and going, and she could not see Jenna. *I'm lost,* Niki thought, and she had a fleeting sensation of what it might feel like if she had dementia and became separated from a loved one.

Niki's experience inspired her to create the "Please don't" section in this chapter. If she were to write something down in that section it would be: *Please don't leave me alone in unfamiliar surroundings.*

About Me

My personality is generally:

(check the personality traits that most apply)

	Happy		Optimistic		Content
	Sad		Pessimistic		Irritable
	Pleasant		Grouchy		Depressed
	Anxious		Extrovert		Introvert
	Fearful		Low energy		High energy
	Paranoid		Assertive		Stubborn

Other: _____

_____

_____

My given name is: _____

I prefer to be called: _____

This is how to demonstrate love to me: _____

_____

_____

_____

My favorite places: _____

_____

_____

_____

I laugh at: _____

_____

_____

_____

This irritates me: _____

_____

_____

_____

I get stressed when: _____

_____

_____

_____

Help me relax by: _____

_____

_____

_____

What makes me happy: _____

_____

_____

_____

What angers me: _____

_____

_____

_____

I have these tics or habits: _____

_____

_____

Don't be surprised if I: _____

_____

_____

I like these group activities: _____

_____

_____

_____

_____

I indulge in these activities:

    Drink alcohol (how much and what kind)

    _____

    _____

    _____

    Smoke or chew (how often and what kind)

    _____

    _____

    _____

    Use recreational drugs (how often and what kind)

    _____

    _____

    _____

It is easier for me to accept help when: _____

_____

_____

_____

_____

I become aggravated when: _____

_____

_____

_____

_____

I prefer to do this alone: _____

_____

_____

_____

_____

I served in the military: _____

    Years: _____

    Branch: _____

    Rank: _____

Economic background: _____

_____

_____

_____

_____

Occupation: _____

_____

_____

_____

_____

I'm a political junkie who prefers: _____

_____

No politics please: _____

_____

Religion is:

    Important to me: _____

    Faith: _____

    Not important: _____

These things scare me:

The dark	Bodies of water	Spiders
Birds	Clowns	Dogs
Cats	Loud sounds	Fireworks
Closed-in spaces	Being alone	Being in crowds
Snakes	Heights	Flying
Thunder/Lightning	Blood	Riding in a car

Other scary things: _____

_____

_____

_____

Trauma I've experienced: _____

_____

_____

_____

_____

_____

_____

_____

Significant losses in my life: _____

_____

_____

_____

_____

_____

What brings value to my life: _____

_____

_____

_____

_____

Ways to make me feel useful: _____

_____

_____

_____

_____

_____

_____

Important dates to remember and why:

_____   _____

_____   _____

_____   _____

_____   _____

_____   _____

_____

What is important to me: _____

_____

_____

_____

_____

_____

Please do: _____

_____

_____

_____

_____

_____

_____

Please don't: _____

_____

_____

_____

_____

_____

_____

Checking in: Date: _____

Describe your thoughts or feelings today:

_____

_____

_____

_____

_____

_____

_____

_____

_____

_____

_____

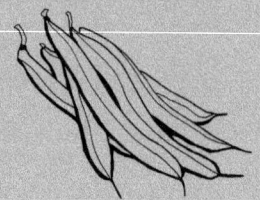

Everyone is different. We all have our preferred food or drink, scents or music, shows we like to watch, or movies that would make us leave the room. Niki's family knows she'll take a rom-com any day over the blockbuster thriller, while Jenna will watch almost anything. Do others know what you like? Let people know what you prefer so that you don't find yourself eating green beans when you'd rather have corn.

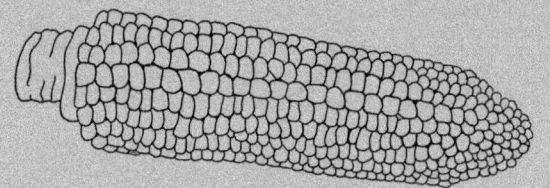

My Preferences

I like

Foods:

_____

_____

_____

_____

_____

_____

_____

_____

_____

I do not like

Foods:

_____

_____

_____

_____

_____

_____

_____

_____

_____

I like

Drinks:

_____

_____

_____

_____

Scents:

_____

_____

_____

Animals:

_____

_____

_____

_____

I do not like

Drinks:

_____

_____

_____

_____

Scents:

_____

_____

_____

Animals:

_____

_____

_____

_____

I like

Flowers:

_____

_____

_____

_____

Holidays:

_____

_____

_____

_____

Sports:

_____

_____

_____

I do not like

Flowers:

_____

_____

_____

_____

Holidays:

_____

_____

_____

_____

Sports:

_____

_____

_____

I like

Activities:

_____

_____

_____

_____

Clothing:

_____

_____

_____

_____

Textures and fabrics:

_____

_____

_____

I do not like

Activities:

_____

_____

_____

_____

Clothing:

_____

_____

_____

_____

Textures and fabrics:

_____

_____

_____

I prefer to be: _____Outdoors _____Indoors

I like: _____Summer _____Winter

_____Spring _____Fall

I'm an:

_____Extrovert _____Introvert

Keep me:

_____Warm _____Cool

I like my feet:

_____With socks _____Shoes on _____Bare

_____I'm modest _____What's a little skin?

_____I'm a neat freak _____Clutter never hurts anyone

_____I'm an early bird _____I'm a night owl

_____I like babies and children _____I'm not fond of strangers

_____I like to be touched and hugged

_____Hands off please

_____I like to share _____Please don't touch my stuff

Favorite Movies:

Favorite TV shows:

Favorite music:

Favorite Restaurants: Preferred meal:

_____   _____

_____   _____

_____   _____

_____   _____

Favorite Fast Foods: Preferred meal:

_____   _____

_____   _____

_____   _____

_____   _____

Favorite Desserts:

_____

_____

_____

_____

Other things I like: _____

_____

_____

_____

_____

_____

_____

Other things I don't like: _____

_____

_____

_____

_____

_____

Checking in: Date: _____

Describe your thoughts or feelings today:

_____

_____

_____

_____

_____

_____

_____

_____

_____

_____

_____

_____

We all have our routines, our favorite way to wake up in the morning or wind down at night. For some, it's that first cup of coffee or the smell of bacon. Niki's father listened to Joan Baez and some of her earliest memories were of Joan's songs on the stereo, letting her know it was time to get up. Niki is a morning person and her day just does not start out right without that morning shower. Jenna, on the other hand, identifies as a night owl and finds mornings to be the most difficult part of the day.

Daily Routine

Morning

Wake up time: _____

Best way to wake me up: _____

_____

Shower or bath: _____ Water temperature: _____

Hair style: _____

Make up: _____

Shave: _____

Favorite products: _____

_____

_____

_____

Breakfast time: _____

_____

Favorite breakfast foods: _____

_____

_____

_____

Activities: _____

_____

_____

Afternoon

Lunch time: _____

Favorite meal: _____

_____

_____

_____

Nap time: _____   Length: _____

Activities: _____

_____

_____

Evening

Dinner time: _____

Favorite meal: _____

_____

_____

_____

_____

Activities: _____

_____

_____

Shower or bath: _____ Water temperature: _____

Bed time: _____

Preferred sleep clothing: _____

_____

_____

_____

Bedroom environment:

Lights	On	Off
Night light	On	Off
Music	On	Off
Television	On	Off
Humidifier	Yes	No
Sound Machine	Yes	No
Fan	Yes	No
Windows	Open	Closed
Door	Open	Closed

_____ I sleep through the night _____ I wake up often

_____ I'm a light sleeper _____ I'm a heavy sleeper

_____ I have night terrors or PTSD

_____ I have pleasant dreams

Checking in: Date: _____

Describe your thoughts or feelings today:

_____

_____

_____

Although Niki is mostly healthy, she suffers from heartburn, so she doesn't eat spicy food or chocolate less than three hours before going to bed. Otherwise, she will pay the price by waking up in the middle of the night with acid reflux. Her future care partner needs to know this if she is unable to tell them herself. What are your health needs or concerns?

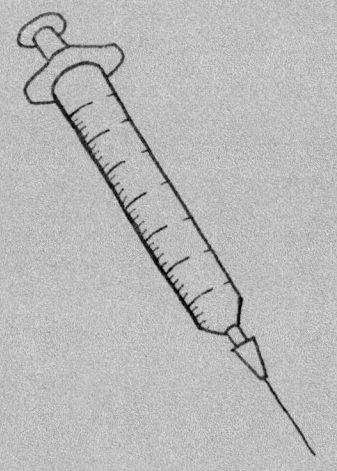

Health and Wellness

Current Medical Conditions:

	Arteriosclerosis		Alzheimer's		Diabetes
	Cardiac Dysrhythmia		Dementia		Cerebral Palsy
	Congestive Heart Failure		Aphasia		Diverticulitis
	Hypertension		Stroke		HIV
	Hypotension		Multiple Sclerosis		Irritable Bowel
	Peripheral Vascular Disease		Parkinson's disease		Osteoporosis
	Emphysema		Arthritis		Seizure Disorder
	Asthma		Cancer		Tuberculosis
	COPD		Pneumonia		GERD
	Hypoglycemia		High cholesterol		Lactose Intolerance
	Mental health		Depression		Anxiety

Other: _____

_____

_____

_____

My bladder is shy: _____

    I frequently urinate: _____

This helps me have a bowel movement: _____

I have bowel movements:

Many times a day_____   Daily_____

Every other day_____   Irregular_____

Surgery	Date

Immunizations:

Type	Date
COVID-19	
Influenza	
Pneumonia	
Shingles	
Tetanus/Tdap	
Other:	

No immunizations please:_____

Best way to take medications: _____

_____

_____

_____

Medication allergies and symptoms:

_____	_____
_____	_____
_____	_____
_____	_____
_____	_____
_____	_____

I am sensitive to pain: _____

_____

_____

I am sensitive to medications: _____

_____

_____

I have these implants: _____

_____

I can have an MRI: _____

_____

Environmental allergies and symptoms:

_____   _____

_____   _____

_____   _____

_____   _____

_____   _____

Food Allergies and Symptoms:

_____   _____

_____   _____

_____   _____

_____   _____

_____   _____

Family health history:

Mother:

Father:

Siblings:

_____   _____

_____   _____

_____   _____

_____   _____

_____   _____

_____   _____

_____   _____

Extended family:

_____   _____

_____   _____

_____   _____

_____   _____

_____   _____

_____I have an advanced directive

_____I have a POLST

If I develop an illness aside from dementia, here are my choices for care:

Condition	Possible Treatments	Always	Never	Doctor Recommendation
Infection	Antibiotics			
Heart	Surgery			
Stroke	Medication			
Brain	Surgery			
Cancer	Surgery			
Cancer	Radiation			
Cancer	Chemotherapy			
Other:				

Life support (feeding tube, ventilator)	Always	Period of time	Never	Doctor Recommendation
If expected to recover				
If irreversible coma/brain damage				
If near death				

Terminal illness	Traditional treatment	Experimental treatment	Comfort care only	Doctor Recommendation
Less than 1 year				
Less than 6 months				
Near death				

_____**My desire is to have full treatment, at any time, under any condition, regardless of prognosis, in an effort to save my life.**

Checking in: Date: _____

Describe your thoughts or feelings today:

_____

_____

_____

_____

_____

_____

_____

_____

_____

_____

When working with seniors, Niki sometimes encounters people who have no children and their spouse, friends, and family have predeceased them. Without living friends and family to share stories, very little is known about the person receiving care. Take a moment to write about your life, growing up years, and family so your care partners can reminisce with you.

My Life

Town I was born in: _____

Towns I lived in and when:

_____   _____

_____   _____

_____   _____

My parents' names: _____

_____

I was:

       an only child_____   the oldest _____

       the middle_____   the youngest_____

Siblings:

_____   _____

_____   _____

_____   _____

Extended family:

_____   _____

_____   _____

_____   _____

I went to high school: _____

I went to college: _____

I studied: _____

Place I met my spouse: _____

Name of spouse: _____

We had children:

_____   _____

_____   _____

_____   _____

We had grandchildren:

_____   _____

_____   _____

_____   _____

Other marriages or significant others:

_____   _____

_____   _____

_____   _____

I had pets:

_____   _____

_____   _____

_____   _____

I worked at: _____

Job title: _____

I worked at: _____

Job title: _____

I worked at: _____

Job title: _____

My favorite place when growing up was: _____

_____

My favorite place as an adult was: _____

_____

My best memory as a child: _____

_____

_____

_____

_____

_____

_____

_____

My best memory as an adult: _____

_____

_____

_____

_____

_____

_____

_____

Checking in: Date: _____

Describe your thoughts or feelings today:

_____

_____

_____

_____

_____

_____

_____

_____

_____

_____

_____

_____

Some changes creep up unexpectedly. Maybe you noticed that you were becoming more forgetful or your family expressed concerns. Perhaps you got lost driving home from the store, a drive you should be able to make with your eyes closed. You decided it was time to see the doctor and anticipated a new vitamin or exercise routine would be prescribed to help. Instead, you were given the most devastating news you had hoped would never be spoken: Dementia.

In this section, describe your feelings as you are facing new challenges, but also focus on how you want to thrive in your "new normal."

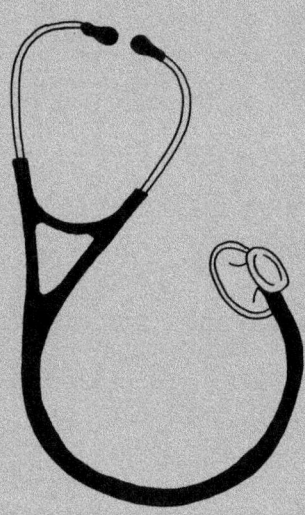

Memory Loss

The day I was diagnosed with dementia: _____

My feelings: _____

_____

_____

_____

_____

_____

_____

_____

_____

_____

_____

People I told: _____

_____

_____

_____

_____

_____

_____

_____

_____

_____

_____

_____

_____

_____

_____

Their reaction: _____

What I am afraid of: _____

_____

_____

_____

_____

_____

_____

_____

_____

_____

_____

_____

_____

_____

_____

What I can still do: _____

What I would like to do while I'm still able: _____

_____

_____

_____

_____

_____

_____

_____

_____

_____

_____

_____

_____

_____

_____

Niki learned to drive her stepfather's truck in the desert at age fourteen, was joyriding in her mother's car at fifteen, and driving legally at sixteen. Her car keys represent freedom and independence. She has often said that her family will need to "pry my keys from my cold dead hands." Really though, she hopes they will know what is best, and that they will do what needs to be done.

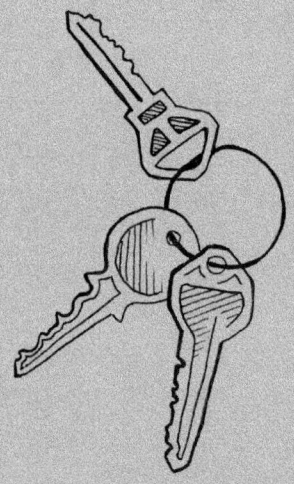

When I Need Care

Home or facility: _____

_____

Facility preference: _____

_____

Care partner preference: _____

_____

_____

If I wander: _____

_____

_____

If I become aggressive: _____

_____

_____

_____

If I can't safely drive any more: _____

_____

_____

Techniques for cooperation: _____

_____

_____

I get confused when: _____

_____

_____

If I require heavy care or am bed-bound: _____

_____

_____

If I'm at risk for falls and injury: _____

_____

_____

Here's how to decorate my room in a facility: _____

_____

_____

Please bring these possessions with me: _____
_____
_____

I have a pet. Please do this: _____
_____
_____

If I'm sundowning: _____
_____
_____

If I'm incontinent: _____
_____
_____

Eye care: _____
_____
_____

Teeth and lips: _____
_____
_____

Skin care: _____

_____

_____

Nail care: _____

_____

_____

Foot care: _____

_____

Hair care: _____

_____

_____

Shaving: _____

_____

Hearing aids: _____

_____

Eyeglasses: _____

_____

Ambulation: _____

Care partner preference:

Male or female: _____ Nurturing or no-nonsense: _____

Young or old: _____

Other preferences: _____

_____

_____

I like to eat: _____ alone in a dining room

_____ alone in my room   _____ with others

Make sure I always have a purse or wallet: _____

with money? _____

I have a gun: _____

It is stored: _____

Important papers are kept: _____

_____

_____

_____

_____

This person knows me best: _____

_____

This person can make decisions for me: _____

_____

Inform me of family deaths: _____

_____

Keep informing me if I ask, or just say they are gone for the day:

_____

_____

Checking in: Date: _____

Describe your thoughts or feelings today:

_____

_____

_____

_____

_____

When it is time, none of us will escape it. Every living being will leave this life in one way or another. While you cannot control that, take a moment to reflect on what you can control—how you want to spend your last days.

Final Days

I want to die: _____at home _____ at a hospice facility

_____in a hospital

I want people around me: _____Yes _____No

It's okay for visitors to laugh and share stories:

_____Yes _____No

Please play this type of music: _____

_____

Please have this type of lighting: _____

_____

Keep the temperature: _____

I want it: _____Quiet _____Noisy _____Moderate

My religious preferences:

_____Please have a spiritual advisor present

_____Please read scripture

_____Please play hymns or praise songs

Please sedate me if I'm in pain: _____

I'll tolerate a little pain to be alert: _____

Let these people know if my time is near:

Name: _____

Contact Information: _____

Name: _____

Contact Information: _____

Name: _____

Contact Information: _____

Name: _____

Contact Information: _____

Name: _____

Contact Information: _____

Name: _____

Contact Information: _____

Checking in: Date: _____

Describe your thoughts or feelings today:

_____

_____

_____

_____

_____

_____

_____

_____

_____

_____

_____

_____

Everyone has a preference on how they want to be remembered. Niki's stepfather asked her mother to "throw one heck of a party." And a grand party it was. Niki's dad asked for "three comely lasses to sing 'Nearer My God to Thee.'" (What he got instead was his daughter, granddaughter, and granddaughter-in-law singing.) If it matters to you, be sure to let others know your wishes.

After I'm Gone

Family/friends to be notified of my passing:

Name: _____

Contact Information: _____

Name: _____

Contact Information: _____

Name: _____

Contact Information: _____

Name: _____

Contact Information: _____

Name: _____

Contact Information: _____

Name: _____

Contact Information: _____

There is a will, located: _____

_____

Executor of my will: _____

Phone Number: _____

Final arrangements:

_____Cremation Prepaid with: _____

_____

Contact: _____

Ashes to be placed or scattered: _____

_____

_____Burial Prepaid with: _____

Contact: _____

Other: _____

_____

_____

_____

_____

Where I would like my service held: _____

_____

_____

Flowers:

_____   _____

_____   _____

Please donate to:

_____   _____

_____   _____

Speakers:

_____   _____

_____   _____

Songs:

_____   _____

_____   _____

Checking in: Date: _____

Describe your thoughts or feelings today:

_____

_____

_____

_____

_____

_____

_____

_____

_____

_____

_____

_____

In previous generations, people left their final words on their gravestone. These days, few people are buried, or if they are, headstones no longer have room to leave last thoughts. Here's your opportunity to share those things that are most important to you.

Last Words

The best thing about my life: _____

_____

_____

_____

_____

_____

_____

_____

_____

_____

My greatest achievement:_____

_____

_____

_____

_____

_____

_____

_____

_____

_____

_____

_____

_____

_____

_____

I accomplished all these things: _____

_____

_____

_____

_____

_____

_____

_____

_____

_____

_____

_____

_____

_____

_____

I wish I had done this: _____

My biggest regret: _____

I will miss this most of all: _____

_____

_____

_____

_____

_____

_____

_____

_____

_____

_____

_____

_____

_____

I want my family to remember me this way:_____

_____

_____

_____

_____

_____

_____

_____

_____

_____

_____

_____

_____

_____

Addendums

So much of our lives are online now: bank accounts, social interactions, bill paying, pictures, and more. When Niki's mom passed away, Niki was fortunate to have access to her mom's laptop logins and passwords. Niki was seamlessly able to pay bills, close accounts, and notify all her mom's friends of her passing. Completing this section will make it easy for those who are helping you—but be sure you trust them!

Technology

Computer login: _____

Phone login: _____

Email: _____

    Password _____

Email: _____

    Password _____

Website: _____

    Purpose _____

    User Name _____

    Password _____

Website: _____

    Purpose _____

    User Name _____

    Password _____

Website: _____

    Purpose _____

    User Name _____

    Password _____

Website: _____

    Purpose _____

    User Name _____

    Password _____

Website: _____

    Purpose _____

    User Name _____

    Password _____

Website: _____

    Purpose _____

    User Name _____

    Password _____

Website: _____

    Purpose _____

    User Name _____

    Password _____

Website: _____

    Purpose _____

    User Name _____

    Password _____

Website: _____

    Purpose _____

    User Name _____

    Password _____

Website: _____

    Purpose _____

    User Name _____

    Password _____

Website: _____

    Purpose _____

    User Name _____

    Password _____

Website: _____

    Purpose _____

    User Name _____

    Password _____

Website: _____

    Purpose _____

    User Name _____

    Password _____

Website: _____

    Purpose _____

    User Name _____

    Password _____

With all that you are going through, you may be making multiple visits to different doctors. Here is a place where you can keep track of when you went, who you saw, and what happened while you were. As a care manager, Niki often escorts seniors to medical appointments to ask questions they might not remember to ask and take notes on what the doctor said. It's always a good idea to have someone go with you for a second pair of ears.

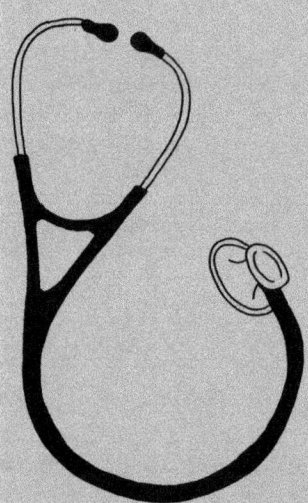

Doctors' Visits

Date: _____ Dr. _____

Purpose: _____

Outcome: _____

_____

_____

_____

Date: _____ Dr. _____

Purpose: _____

Outcome: _____

_____

_____

_____

Date: _____   Dr. _____

Purpose: _____

Outcome: _____

_____

_____

_____

_____

_____

Date: _____   Dr. _____

Purpose: _____

Outcome: _____

_____

_____

_____

_____

_____

Date: _____ Dr. _____

Purpose: _____

Outcome: _____

_____

_____

_____

_____

Date: _____ Dr. _____

Purpose: _____

Outcome: _____

_____

_____

_____

_____

Date: _____   Dr. _____

Purpose: _____

Outcome: _____

_____

_____

_____

_____

Date: _____   Dr. _____

Purpose: _____

Outcome: _____

_____

_____

_____

_____

Date: _____   Dr. _____

Purpose: _____

Outcome: _____

_____

_____

_____

_____

Date: _____   Dr. _____

Purpose: _____

Outcome: _____

_____

_____

_____

_____

Date: _____   Dr. _____

Purpose: _____

Outcome: _____

_____

_____

_____

_____

_____

Date: _____   Dr. _____

Purpose: _____

Outcome: _____

_____

_____

_____

_____

_____

Date: _____   Dr. _____

Purpose: _____

Outcome: _____

_____

_____

_____

_____

Date: _____   Dr. _____

Purpose: _____

Outcome: _____

_____

_____

_____

_____

Date: _____ Dr. _____

Purpose: _____

Outcome: _____

_____

_____

_____

_____

_____

Date: _____ Dr. _____

Purpose: _____

Outcome: _____

_____

_____

_____

_____

_____

Date: _____   Dr. _____

Purpose: _____

Outcome: _____

_____

_____

_____

_____

Date: _____   Dr. _____

Purpose: _____

Outcome: _____

_____

_____

_____

_____

Date: _____   Dr. _____

Purpose: _____

Outcome: _____

_____

_____

_____

_____

_____

Date: _____   Dr. _____

Purpose: _____

Outcome: _____

_____

_____

_____

_____

_____

Date: _____   Dr. _____

Purpose: _____

Outcome: _____

_____

_____

_____

_____

_____

Date: _____   Dr. _____

Purpose: _____

Outcome: _____

_____

_____

_____

_____

_____

Along with doctor visits, you may find that new medications are tried and others stopped. Keep track of your changes in medications and note down what works for you and what doesn't. When Niki's dad was in the hospital being treated for pneumonia, his doctor prescribed anxiety medication to calm his agitation. Unfortunately, the drug prescribed only increased his anxiety so much that he wanted to remove his IV and get out of bed. It is important to record both positive and negative effects you have experienced from medications.

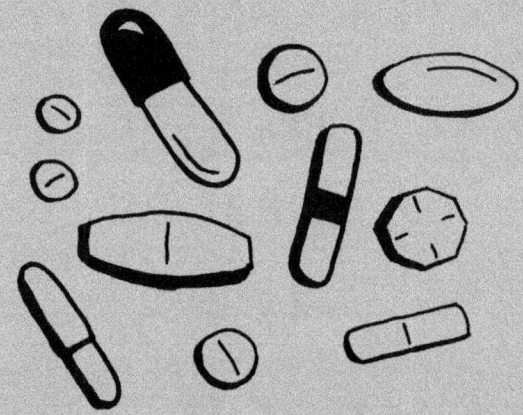

Medication List

Date: _____

New medication: _____

Discontinued medication: _____

Why the change:_____

_____

_____

_____

Date: _____

New medication: _____

Discontinued medication: _____

Why the change:_____

_____

_____

_____

Date: _____

New medication: _____

Discontinued medication: _____

Why the change: _____

_____

_____

_____

Date: _____

New medication: _____

Discontinued medication: _____

Why the change: _____

_____

_____

_____

Date: _____

New medication: _____

Discontinued medication: _____

Why the change: _____

_____

_____

_____

Date: _____

New medication: _____

Discontinued medication: _____

Why the change: _____

_____

_____

_____

Date: _____

New medication: _____

Discontinued medication: _____

Why the change: _____

_____

_____

_____

Date: _____

New medication: _____

Discontinued medication: _____

Why the change: _____

_____

_____

_____

Date: _____

New medication: _____

Discontinued medication: _____

Why the change:_____

_____

_____

_____

Date: _____

New medication: _____

Discontinued medication: _____

Why the change:_____

_____

_____

_____

Date: _____

New medication: _____

Discontinued medication: _____

Why the change: _____

_____

_____

_____

Date: _____

New medication: _____

Discontinued medication: _____

Why the change: _____

_____

_____

_____

Date: _____

New medication: _____

Discontinued medication: _____

Why the change: _____

_____

_____

_____

Date: _____

New medication: _____

Discontinued medication: _____

Why the change: _____

_____

_____

_____

Date: _____

New medication: _____

Discontinued medication: _____

Why the change: _____

_____

_____

_____

Date: _____

New medication: _____

Discontinued medication: _____

Why the change: _____

_____

_____

_____

Date: _____

New medication: _____

Discontinued medication: _____

Why the change: _____

_____

_____

_____

Date: _____

New medication: _____

Discontinued medication: _____

Why the change: _____

_____

_____

_____

With all the changes, you may be feeling fearful and regretful, or holding on tight to the wonderful things you are doing today. Consider keeping a diary as you travel this path so that others may follow this journey behind you.

Diary

Date: _____

_____

_____

_____

_____

_____

_____

Date: _____

_____

_____

_____

_____

_____

_____

Date: _____

_____

_____

_____

_____

_____

_____

_____

Date: _____

_____

_____

_____

_____

_____

_____

_____

Date: _____

_____

_____

_____

_____

_____

_____

_____

_____

Date: _____

_____

_____

_____

_____

_____

_____

_____

_____

Date: _____

_____

_____

_____

_____

_____

_____

_____

Date: _____

_____

_____

_____

_____

_____

_____

_____

Date: _____

_____

_____

_____

_____

_____

_____

_____

Date: _____

_____

_____

_____

_____

_____

_____

_____

Date: _____

Date: _____

Date: _____

_____

_____

_____

_____

_____

_____

_____

Date: _____

_____

_____

_____

_____

_____

_____

_____

Date: _____

_____

_____

_____

_____

_____

_____

_____

Date: _____

_____

_____

_____

_____

_____

_____

_____

Date: _____

_____

_____

_____

_____

_____

_____

_____

Date: _____

_____

_____

_____

_____

_____

_____

_____

Date: _____

Date: _____

Date: _____

_____

_____

_____

_____

_____

_____

_____

Date: _____

_____

_____

_____

_____

_____

_____

_____

Date: _____

_____

_____

_____

_____

_____

_____

_____

Date: _____

_____

_____

_____

_____

_____

_____

_____

Date: _____

Date: _____

Date: _____

_____

_____

_____

_____

_____

_____

_____

Date: _____

_____

_____

_____

_____

_____

_____

_____

Date: _____

_____

_____

_____

_____

_____

_____

_____

Date: _____

_____

_____

_____

_____

_____

_____

_____

Date: _____

_____

_____

_____

_____

_____

_____

_____

Date: _____

_____

_____

_____

_____

_____

_____

_____

Acknowledgements by Niki:

My husband Jim
who said of all the "thousands" of ideas I've had over the years,
this was better than all the others put together
Thank you for encouraging me

My children:
Jimmy, Jenna,
Joey and Sarah
Shaun and Megan
Thank you for your love

Cy Osborne, my business partner and
his very tolerant wife Carol
I do so listen to you.
Thank you for your advice

Deb Hubbell, my "bestie" and her husband Gene
No one makes me laugh more than you
Thank you for your shoulder to cry and laugh on

My brother Mark Morris and his wife Beth
We could not have done it
without your input and feedback

Their son Eamon
For his great artwork

Luminare Press
For putting our dream into reality

Thanks also to the many others who encouraged, advised
and listened to us. We are very grateful for your assistance.

Acknowledgements by Jenna:

Thank you to the Clark County Training Center
and Melinda Grooms-Unruh
For teaching me the skills necessary for caring for seniors

Thank you to Touchmark at Fairway Village
For five great years of experience.

www.ingramcontent.com/pod-product-compliance
Lightning Source LLC
LaVergne TN
LVHW081528060526
838200LV00045B/2035